Bushfire Ready

Michelle Vasiliu

Australia • Brazil • Japan • Korea • Mexico • Singapore • Spain • United Kingdom • United States

Bushfire Ready

Text: Michelle Vasiliu
Editor: Vanessa Pellatt
Design: Kerri Wilson
Series design: James Lowe
Photo researcher: Libby Henry
Production controllers: Renee Cusmano and Lisa Porter
Reprint: Jennifer Foo

Acknowledgements
The author and publisher would like to acknowledge permission to reproduce material from the following sources:
AAP Image/Dan Peled: p. 5; AAP Image/Kerri Kingston: p. 21; AAP Image/Simon Renilson: p. 23 (bottom); Andrew Louey © Cengage Learning Australia: p. 4; Auscape/John Carnemolla: p. 4 (inset); Corbis Australia: pp. 7, 16, 19 (inset); Fairfaxphotos/Pat Scala: p. 6 (main); Fairfaxphotos/Simon O'Dwyer: p. 9; Fotolia/Freeze Frame Photography: p. 18 (bottom left); Fotolia/martin3174140496: p. 18 (top); Getty Images: pp. 1, 3, 4 (background), 8, 10 (middle), 13, 14, 17 (left), cover, back cover; iStockphoto/Slobo Mitic: p. 22 (top right); Newspix/Amy Brown: p. 10 (bottom); Newpix/David Crosling: pp. 11 (main), 20 (bottom); Newspix/James Kerr: p. 19 (main); Newspix/Kim Eiszele: p. 12; Newspix/Quest Papers: p. 23 (top left); Photolibrary: pp. 6 (inset), 10 (top), 17 (right), 18 (bottom right), 20 (top), 22 (bottom), 23 (top right); Shutterstock/Alexander Kalina: p. 11 (bottom right); Shutterstock/Chrislofoto: p. 22 (top left); Shutterstock/jocicalek: p. 15 (lawnmower); Shutterstock/Laurie Barr: p. 15 (rake); Shutterstock/Mikko Pitkänen: p. 15 (bucket); Shutterstock/objectsforall: p. 15 (hose); Shutterstock/Rob Byron: p. 11 (bottom left).

Page 4: Illustration based on a map from the Bureau of Meterology, © Copyright Commonwealth of Australia 2008.

Fast Forward Independent Texts
Level 20

For product information and technology assistance,
in Australia call 1300 790 853;
in New Zealand call 0508 635 766

For permission to use material from this text or product,
please email **aust.permissions@cengage.com**

ISBN 978 0 17 017941 6
ISBN 978 0 17 017898 3 (set)

Cengage Learning Australia
Level 7, 80 Dorcas Street
South Melbourne, Victoria Australia 3205

Cengage Learning New Zealand
Unit 4B Rosedale Office Park
331 Rosedale Road, Albany, North Shore NZ 0632

For learning solutions, visit **cengage.com.au**

Printed in Australia by Ligare Pty Ltd
2 3 4 5 6 7 8 21 20 19 18 17

Michelle Vasiliu

Contents

CHAPTER 1

Bushfires

Bushfires are common in Australia. Most bushfires happen in the hot summer months.

But in some areas bushfires happen during spring, autumn or winter. They can be started by people or by **lightning**.

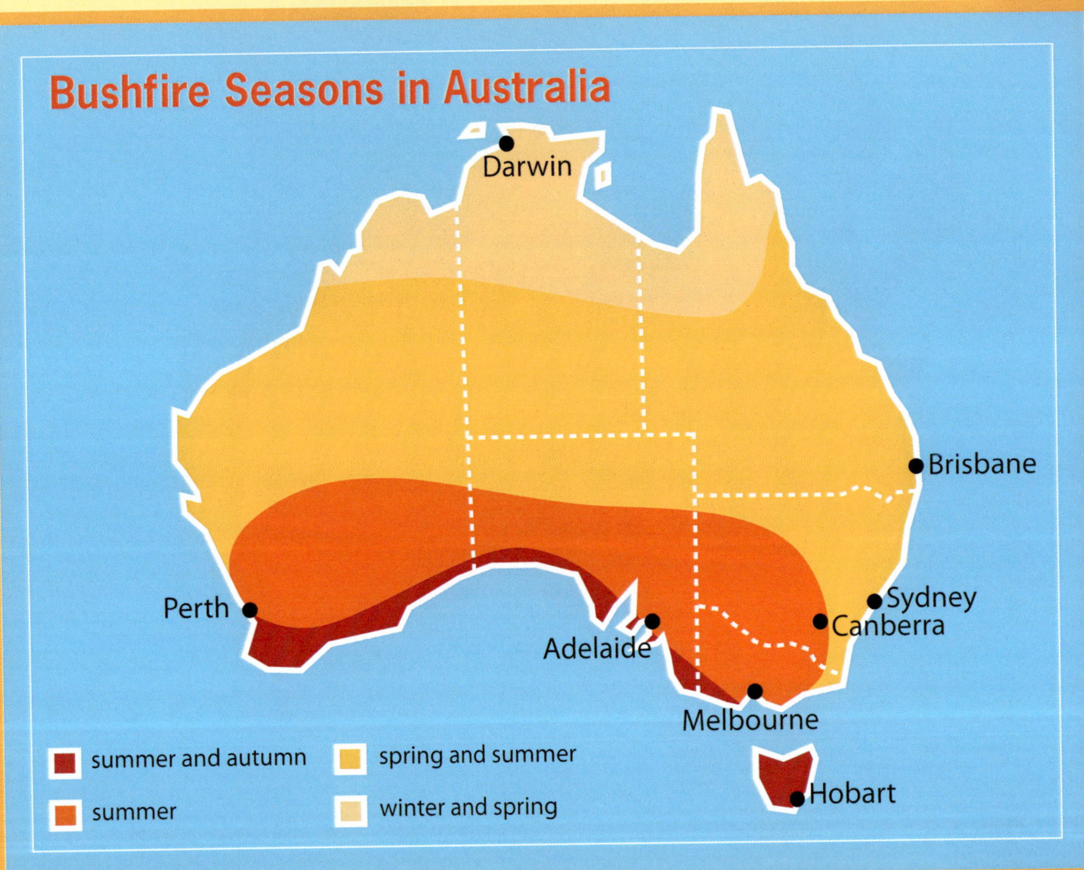

In dry conditions, bushfires move across the land quickly, putting homes, buildings, crops, farm animals, forests and **wildlife** in danger.

Sometimes bushfires are so big it is hard to control them.

This helicopter is dumping water on a bushfire.

CHAPTER 2

Bushfire Safety

The fire-fighting authorities are not always able to protect every home.

Every state has volunteers who help fight bushfires.

So it is important that people who live in the bush know what to do in bushfire season.

FIRE DANGER TODAY
LOW
MODERATE
HIGH
VERY HIGH
EXTREME
NO FIRES WITHOUT A PERMIT

Experts recommend
that people make a "Bushfire Survival Plan".

This plan should set out what to do
on days that have a high fire-risk.
Everyone in the family should know the plan.
They should understand
what to do if a bushfire starts.
They should practise the plan
before they need to use it.

The Bushfire Survival Plan helps people decide if they should leave their property or stay and fight the fire.

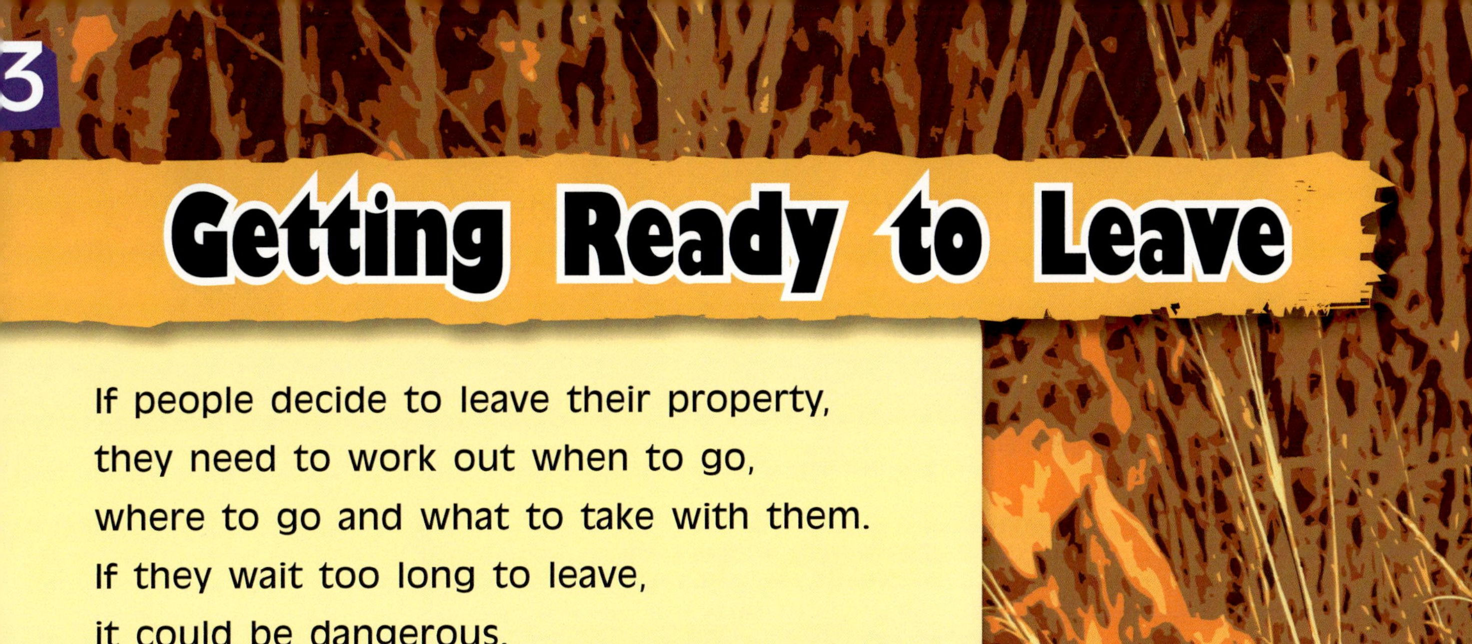

Getting Ready to Leave

If people decide to leave their property, they need to work out when to go, where to go and what to take with them. If they wait too long to leave, it could be dangerous.

The decision to leave should be made before the fire gets too close.

These things should be done before leaving:

- Close all windows and doors.
- Collect family members, pets and valuables.
- Tell someone that the family has left and how to reach them.

The decision to leave should be made before the fire gets too close and while the roads are still clear.

Getting Ready to Stay

If people decide to stay to defend their property, they need equipment and supplies to help protect themselves, their families and their homes.

safety goggles

face mask

Wearing long pants will help protect the skin from being burnt.

These things should be done before the fire arrives:

- Put on protective clothes.
- Bring pets inside the house.
- Close all windows and doors.
- Drink plenty of water.
- Fill buckets and containers with extra water.
- Hose down the outside of the house.
- Prepare fire-fighting equipment.
- Listen to the news for fire updates.

CHAPTER 5

How to Get Ready for Bushfire Season

A Bushfire Survival Plan helps people decide if they should stay or go once the bushfire season has started. But there are other things that need to be done well before the bushfire season begins.

Aim:

To protect a house from a bushfire.

Materials:

- lawnmower
- leaf guards
- fire guards or wire mesh
- hoses, mops, buckets
- rakes, shovels, ladders
- full water tank
- working **water pump**
- **backpack sprays**.

Steps:

1. Reduce fine fuels

All plants can be **fuel** for a bushfire. Fine fuels such as dry grass, small sticks, leaves and **bark** burn and give out heat quickly.

- Cut lawns to no less than 50 millimetres high. If green lawns are cut too short they can become dry. A dry lawn can burn very quickly and soon get out of control.

- Cut back plants and trees to stop small fires from getting bigger.

- Replace any **woodchips** in the garden beds with sand or rocks as these will not catch fire.
- Get rid of weeds and clear away dry leaves and bark from around the house.

2. Move other fuels

Make sure fuel and chemicals are kept away from the house.

- Keep wood piles at a safe distance from the house.
- Get rid of any paper from around the outside of the house.
- Keep chemicals and fuel supplies away from the house.

3. Keep the house safe from ember attack

Embers are small burning sticks and leaves.
They are carried by the wind
before the main fire arrives.
They can land on or around the house
and may burn for many hours.
Fires can start up again
if embers are not put out.

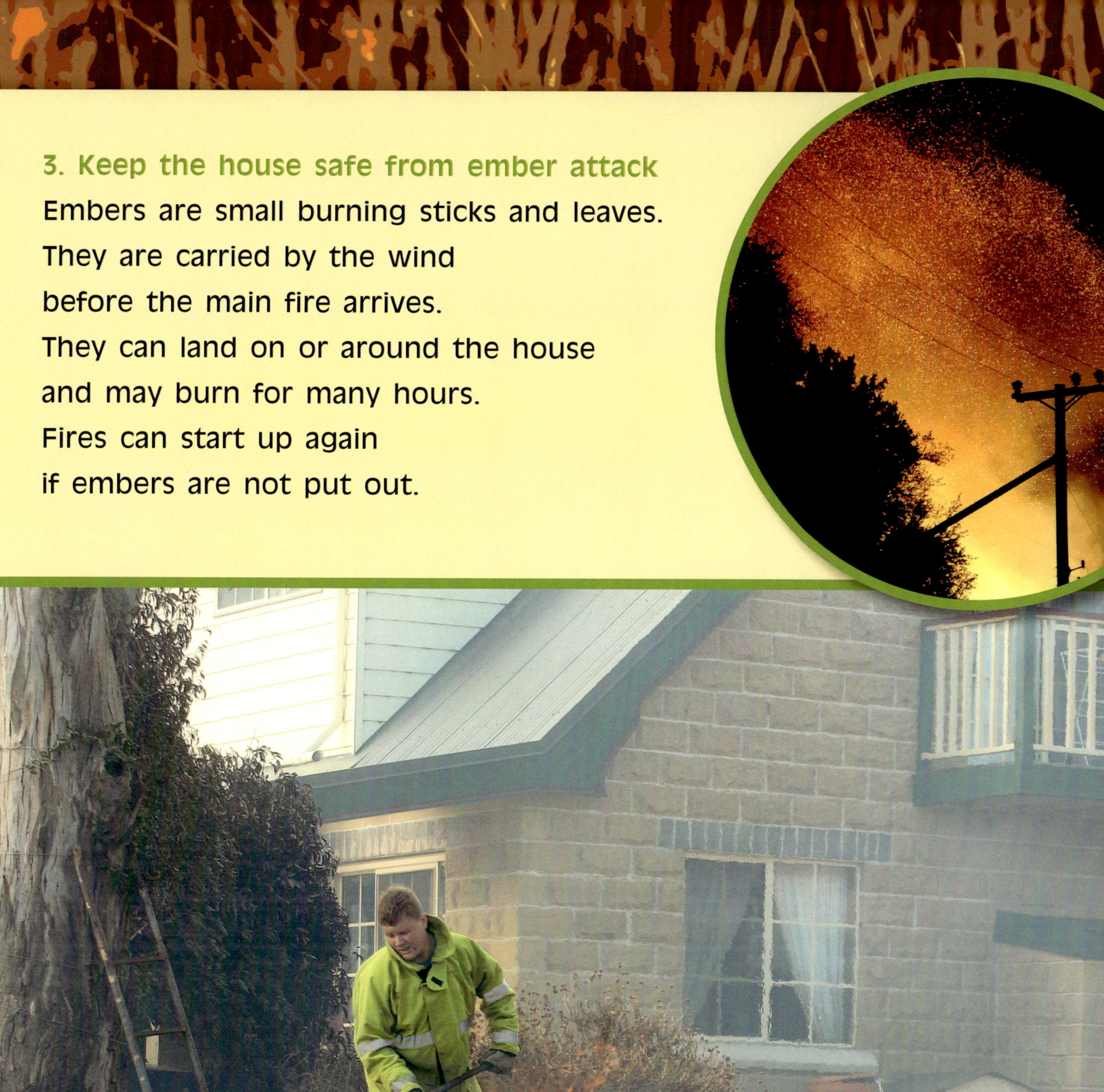

To help control an ember attack

- clean leaves out of the gutters or fit a leaf guard
- put a fire guard or wire mesh over outside openings, windows and doors
- seal all gaps around windows and doors.

Embers can burn for six hours or more.
Many houses burn down
after the main fire has passed
because embers were not put out.

4. Have fire-fighting equipment ready

- Keep fire-fighting equipment such as hoses, buckets, shovels and ladders in easy reach of the house.
- Check that all fire-fighting equipment works.

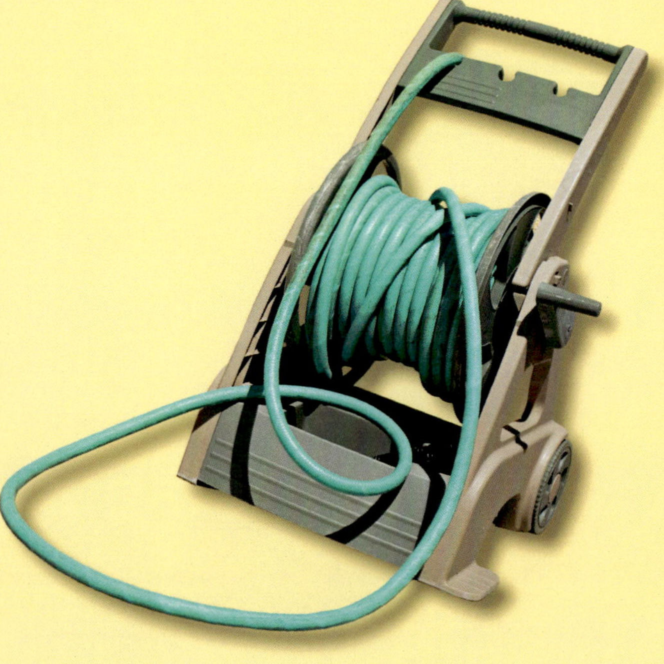

5. Have lots of water on hand

It is important to have other water supplies, as tap water may be cut off in a bushfire.

The water in this swimming pool can be used during a bushfire.

fixing a water pump

- Keep water in big containers, tanks and **dams**.
- Check that water pumps are working.
- Buy or make a backpack spray to carry water for putting out small fires and embers.

A house will stand a much better chance in a bushfire if these steps are followed.

Glossary

backpack spray a backpack containing water with a spray attached, used for putting out small fires

bark the outside of the trunk of a tree

dams water storage areas on a farm

fuel material for burning

lightning a sudden flash of light and electricity in a storm

water pump a machine that moves water through a pipe

wildlife animals living in their natural habitat

woodchips small bits of wood that can be used in garden beds

Index